Extra Cash

Earn Money On The Side And Learn

How You Can Get Paid In Your Spare

Time When You Only Have 20 Dollars

To Spend

by

Lucas Arquette

All contents protected by copyright

law.

Table of Contents:

Chapter 1:

10 Reasons To Make an Extra Income

Introduction

There's no feeling like starting a business, and every year, hundreds of thousands of new businesses are started with hopes of transforming skills and dreams into profits. Sadly, businesses can cost upwards of millions of dollars to get started and most people don't even have a couple of grand in the bank that they can dedicate to starting a new business.

Luckily, there are a couple of ways to start a business that won't break your bank. In fact, you can easily start a profitable business for only $20. While that may seem like a fairy tail dream, millions of people have started their businesses from scratch. In today's world, all it takes to become successful is an internet connection, a belief in yourself and an understanding of how to capitalize on your opportunities and skills to spark some initial profit.

While these strategies do take time and work to accomplish successfully starting a business, anyone can find a way to build an income without investing money that will break the bank. This book will introduce you to the types of businesses you can build cheaply as well as the mindset, skills and resources needed to accomplish your goals.

There are endless opportunities to start a business around the world. All it takes is confidence and dedication to get started. Many readers want to start a business, but they ultimately give up on their ambitions before they replace their income through business. This book is designed to give you everything you need to get started and launch your first income through business.

In this quick but effective guide you'll be introduced to the types of businesses you can start for $20, how to set up your business, and how to acquire your first sale. Enjoy the journey and if you find yourself with any questions, feel free to do some research online. You'll find tons of free information from professionals looking to give you great information in the hopes that you'll profit from their teachings.

When you find someone who gives you information you profit from, you'll find that they have more advanced programs you can purchase to expand your business and boost your sales. Never be afraid to invest money inside of your business after you start generating income, and have fun while you're kick starting your success!

Cheers to your future success! We'll begin our journey with 10 reasons why starting your own business is the most grand thing you can do for your career, we'll talk about the new mindset you need to develop to succeed in the world of business, and then we'll transition into the wonderful ways you can build a full time income with a simple $20 investment.

Chapter 1:

10 Reasons To Make an Extra Income

There's no better feeling than becoming your own boss, but before you dive into the strategies that will generate sales, it's important to understand why you're passionate about starting your own business. The truth is irrefutable. You're going to spend a large portion of your life working, so why not work for yourself?

Presented below are the 10 most wonderful aspects for starting a business. INC.com recently conducted a survey that included over 450 responses from business owners around the world, and these are the most common benefits that come with being your own boss.

1. You Are Responsible For Your Own Fate.

One of the most powerful aspects about becoming a business owner is understanding that you are in control of the important decisions that will guide your business into the future. When you create a powerful compaction of your personalized business strategies, you'll find that you're naturally good at making profitable decisions once you get into a groove. Do what your passionate about and love your life dearly. There's nothing more powerful than controlling your own destiny throughout your career.

To get yourself started, you can ask yourself these questions to spark a fire under your decision making.

What opportunities would you like to capitalize on?

Where would you like to spend your time?

How would you like to build and expand your business?

What are your ambitions and goals for your company?

Remember that the moment you start your business, you're solely responsible for its success and that's actually a very exciting prospect. By making correct decisions, you'll find yourself making better money in less time. And what's better than being in the driver's seat?

2. You Create Your Own Schedule

One of the coolest parts about running your own business is the ability to set your own schedule. You can choose when and where you'd like to work and the only end to your flexibility is your imagination. If you'd like to hangout with your dog or cat, you can spend time with them while your working away! Running your own business is incredible because it helps you balance out your life after you have the income rolling in. If you'd like to extend your weekend vacation, you can spend a couple of hours of work anywhere in the world, and enjoy the rest of your day.

When you're running your own business, you'll always be able to make time for important events and you'll be able to enjoy the leisure of wearing your favorite clothes when you do choose to work. The perks of owning your own business can be endless, but working with your own schedule is by far one of the best parts of running your business

3. You Get to Hire Your Co-Workers.

When you spend your career working for someone else's business, you're bound to the people you work with, and the only thing you can do to change the situation is to quit and start different job. This can make working with others unbearable if you aren't enjoying the company of your fellow employees.

On the other hand, when you run your own company you get to choose who joins your team and if your employees aren't doing their job, you can shuffle up your crew and cut a bad worker loose. Finding and building a strong team is pretty fun and you can mix things up any time. Having a team that boosts your confidence and transforms your business is pure magic. You can eliminate the negative aspects about working with pessimists and you can build your own culture of positive energy throughout your entire business.

4. The Better You Do, The More You Get Paid.

Although this seems like a pretty obvious perk to running a business, the importance of your performance is often overlooked by new business owners. When you work a standard 9-5 job, you'll find your performance means next to nothing over a period of time. Sure, if you do the right things, you can earn a raise and get a couple of promotions, but all to often it feels like it doesn't actually matter how hard you work. In turn, it's easy to find yourself showing up, doing what is necessary throughout the week, and going home after another casual day in the cruise lane.

On the other hand, owning your own business takes your efforts to an entirely new level. If you produce $1,000 in sales over an hour, you get to keep way more profits than if you made the same amount sales over a week. This situation can bring out the best in your efforts at work. If you're spending 8 hours of your day running your business, you might as well try to make as much money as possible right? The game of business will make work a game and will make every work day more enjoyable. When you control your own income, there's no cap to your income. That in itself is a reason to celebrate!After a couple of months, you'll find yourself eliminating bad conditions for your company while maximizing on the opportunities you have in front of you. Working for your own income puts you into the zone and there's no better way to boost your production than through pushing yourself to the next level.

5. You Have an Opportunity To Push Your Limits of What's Possible.

If you enjoy the daily routine of cruising through your workday without a challenge, starting your own business might not be for you. Running a business pushes the limits of what you can accomplish inside of your life and every week presents a new challenge to conquer. By running your own company, you'll consistently encounter new situations and you'll have to adapt to what's happening or you'll struggle. Owning a business is fun. It constantly presents new ideas and stimulates your mind for success. While you run your business, you'll find that you are consistently adding new skills into your arsenal while you expand your company. Every day, you'll get to learn something new and apply it to your business and your life. Becoming a business owner isn't for everyone, but if you're ready to challenge yourself owning a business will quickly transform your life for the better.

6. You Have A Chance To Do What You Love.

If you've ever hit overtime at work, it feels like the week will never end. It's really easy to get frustrated with how much work you put in because you're likely working for a job that you aren't necessarily enjoying. But when you start your own business, you have a chance to focus on the things you truly love. When you're running your own business, you'll find yourself working more. Instead of time moving in slow motion, you'll find that the weeks pass by and you'll wonder where the time went every month. This is the perfect situation to put yourself in when you start a business.

Ask yourself, "If I could run any business, what would it be?" Even if you can't successfully start your dream business with $20, you can start a business that's a perfect first step to your dream. By having an ability to work on something you love, your odds for success will skyrocket. Plus, if you're choosing to build your own business, why not do something you love? You're going to spend most of your life working, so why not spend your life making a difference in something you truly care about.

7. By Controlling Your Work Flow, You Can Accomplish More In Less Time.

The truth of the matter is that business is run off of things that get done. You can't make a single dime until you complete a series of actions that allow you to complete your first transaction. Luckily for you, you're in complete control over how and when essential actions get done. Another really cool benefit to starting your own business is that when you control your schedule about something your passionate about, you can streamline your productivity and get things done in a flash. When you dive into your work as you launch your business, you'll realize that you're actually quite skilled in creating a service that will positively impact your customers. This is because you know the ins and outs of your business.

When you first start your business, you have a huge competitive edge over large corporations. You have a specific idea to tap into the market and it only takes simplistic action to get things done. Running a business you love will allow you to get things done so you can spend more time doing what you love, and less time in the office.

8. You Can Spend More Time Understanding Your Customers.

When you first start a business, you have the incredible opportunity to understand more about your customers. Most businesses are far too busy to pay special attention to the wants and needs of their clients, but by being able to pay specialized attention to your clients you'll gain a competitive edge over you competition. When you start a business you care about, you'll begin to attract customers who have the same passions and excitement towards what your selling. This creates an environment where you can generate regulars and referrals for your business. By investing in making friendships with your customers, you'll begin to build frequent sales.

And if you don't like one your customers, you can simply do business with them in a polite fashion and show them the door. When you run your business, you're in control of who you do business with and how to show them the proper attention. No one can control your work flow but you. And luckily, a part of business work flow is building a really cool customer base.

9. You Can Make A Positive Impact In Your Community.

A lot of businesses have been started with a mission to make the world a better place. As you business starts to build some nice momentum, you'll begin to notice that you're putting smiles on the faces of your customers. Sometimes, people can be in a pretty tough bind and by providing the right service, you can turn someone's week around in a single hour. And as your company expands, you can sponsor community drives and events. You can even begin hiring employees to expand your impact further. It's nice being able to control whether or not your workplace can help others and owning a small business can be a big deal throughout your community.

10. Small Business Owners Make Their Own Way.

The last perk of starting your own business is the sense of honor that naturally develops when you build something yourself. There's nothing more special in your career than the first time you take your idea and bring it to life. Starting a business provides you with challenges and skills that you never thought you handle. After your business takes shape, it'll become your pride and joy.

Chapter 2:

10 Steps To Making This Work For You

1. Business Is a Marathon To Long Term Success. It's Not a Sprint To a Short Term Fix.

The most fundamental rule to starting a business is to be prepared to be in it for a while. Mastering profits in your business isn't about hitting your first 1K as fast as possible. It's about building a sustainable long term business model that pays your bills for years to come. As you start you business, you'll quickly begin to understand that it isn't for the faint of heart. And it isn't for the skilled professional that isn't prepared to put in consistent work.

When you dive into the realm of business, you'll begin to understand that there are complexities that will take months and even years to build. Thankfully, this doesn't sacrifice initial profit. You're going to find someone who's willing to give you a shot while you build your business from the ground up, but this doesn't mean that your business is built like the Kentucky Derby. You're looking to build a business portfolio that's similar to a triathlon.

It's OK to build your business over time, but there shouldn't ever be a week or month where you shouldn't try to grow and improve your business. The first time you pay your bills through your business will be heaven, but it doesn't mean that you don't have room to grow. Business has no boundaries, and the only limit is your mindset.

Seasoned business owners understand that wealth and success are built over time, and wealth is built over a long term focus on practical implementation of how much money you can make for every hour your business is in operation.

2. $/hour Is The God of Business.

The 9-5 work schedule has plagued the modern era. Once you've acquired a skill set, you can live your life contently as long as you show up and finish the job you were hired for.

The world of business is far different. The only measure of income that exists is how much money you produce for every hour you spend with your business. It's hard to grasp the complexities of business if you look at the world from the perspective that if you show up, you make money. Business is completely different. When a sale is made, you get paid, but if a sale isn't made, you don't. Luckily, a generating a sale is natural and casual. It's just like showing up to work and doing your job. Your first couple of sales are actually pretty easy, but the gravity of action is crucial inside of business.

3. Speed of Implementation.

It's believed by the most successful business owners in the world that speed of implementation inside of an idea is the most fundamental aspect of business. If you don't implement your idea to start a revolutionary business, it's a million times less effective than a business owner who executes on a simple business plan.

Implementation is the most fundamental principle of how much money you generate for every hour that you spend in building your business. Without execution, your business is only a daydream. With action, you live a life of freedom to operate your business by only spending 20 bucks.

4. Keep Yourself Accountable For Your

Production.

When results matter, it's really easy to blame external conditions for production. Running a business on your own schedule is a complicated balance between your physical needs and the dreams that exist in your heart, mind and soul.

When business turns south, it's really easy to blame conditions for business production. "Tomorrow will be better." doesn't work when building a business. Every day counts and nothing is more important than production. In order to keep a business in check, successful owners typically undergo a daily, weekly and monthly check for business production.

They don't look for hard work, but instead they look for production, new opportunities, and ways to improve their current work flow. Without building analytics to measure production, successful businesses models can easily collapse. The amount of money a business owner makes for every hour of work rules the world of small businesses and corporations alike.

5. Test And Measure Everything You

Learn.

Starting a business with little money means that a quick and successful implementation of proven business practice is law.

There are more ways to start a successful business that a single entrepreneur can handle. In order to become successful, new business owners look to seasoned professionals so that they can model proven business tactics. Reinventing the wheel is a massacre to production, and one of the most fundamental aspects of business is you can't improve what you don't inspect. Inspection, or business analytics, are one of the few rulers of success in small businesses and corporations alike.

Learning is production and you're reading this book because you're starting a business. That means that the time spent reading this book must be measured in proportion to the time it takes to successfully start your business by investing only $20.

Begin to apply everything you learn and ensure you measure everything you apply. By using analytics as your key tool as you launch your business, you'll exponentially cut your learning curves.

6. Sacrifice Everything But Your Core Business Principles.

Business revolves around the customer. The customer is always right barring one principle. Vision and core values trump you current customer's belief in your company's future. However, successful business law states that the customer's response to your product is crucial; so how in the world do we balance our vision with our customer's desires? By bridging your market's(you prospective customer base) with your core vision.

By understanding your market's "core desires", you can make your company's vision a reality. All you have to do is find a way to plug in the core values of your business's future into what your customers want.

In other words, sacrifice and compromise on everything other than your vision of your business. Learn how to plug your grand idea into the wants of your market and you'll begin to spark the key to success in business. Innovation.

7. Focus On Innovation More Than Improvement

When someone starts a business, it's almost always because they were inspired by a better future. However, this future can only be created through understanding what the customer cherishes.

In turn, innovation must be used to successfully launch a business, and innovation inside of your market is sparked through creativity. The businesses in this book can all be started without breaking the bank. In order to spark innovation inside of you business it's suggested to look into the Borrow Genius method.

8.   Always Offer What Customers Want.

It's easy to feel like you have the magic key to your industry when you start you business. However, this assumption is a caution flag that is raised most successful business owners. Having a vision is crucial to starting a successful business, but people have to want what you're selling. It's easy to overestimate the success of the ideas you think will be successful; but no matter how good a product is it won't be successful unless it's accepted by the market.

9. Marketing Is The Breath Of Your Business.

In business, nothing happens until you pull in a sale and all of your efforts for nothing if you can't get someone to pull the trigger on whatever you're offering. Many people begin their journey through business with the approach that they should build their brand and their products before they focus on getting their first customer. And while this naturally sounds like a sound business approach, it's the wrong way to go about business. As your business launches, having a way to acquire and engage with perspective clients

Marketing is the breath of every business and it allows a new business owner to understand what customers find most important and to provide a service that can help your customers in ways you never thought. By starting your business through marketing you'll be able to find more prospective customers quickly and you'll be able to present your products in ways that your market responds well to.

10. Don't Improve Your Industry, Innovate It.

When you go in to start your business, try to transform whatever area you're looking for. Don't look at a way to become a little bit better than your competition. As your marketing, really dive into your customer and understand what they are looking for. Then look at your vision for your company and try to find a way to innovate you products and services in a way that isn't currently being done.

When you supply clients with something new, it generates buzz and excitement around your product lines. Even if you don't understand how marketing works right out of the gate, you'll quickly begin to learn how marketing works. When everything is stripped down to its bear bones, marketing is about finding something that customers want, understand why they want it, develop a marketing strategy that triggers your potential customers, and to casually close a sale through presenting an offer.

Now that you understand how great running your own business is and more about the underlying principles that make a business launch successful, it's time to dive into the businesses that can be started for $20.

Chapter 3:

Businesses That Can Be Started With $20 or Less

Starting a business is pretty exciting and you'll be surprised at how many businesses you can actually start of under $20. Cruise through these ideas and try to find a gap you can fill so you can start your dream business down the road.

Here are a series of businesses you can start with no money as collateral. These businesses can all be started by anyone with a tight budget.

1. **Become a Meal Planning Consultant.**

Meal planning services have been taking off over the past couple of years and now is the perfect time to hop on to the bandwagon. If you love cooking and you have a stash of recipes for healthy diets or holiday menus, this might be the perfect job for you! Many people enjoy cooking great meals, but they don't want to spend their time planning out every meal. By sending out weekly and monthly meal plans and grocery lists, you'll begin to gain traction and start generating sales from people who are too busy to plan everything out. The types of diets that are available are endless, but double check best selling recipe books and frequently visited websites to make sure your specialty works.

Easy Steps to becoming a meal plan consultant for $20.

Step 1: Identify your meal plan topics. Specialize on 3 popular diets and you can mix in a holiday meal plan if you'd like to! Just make sure that what you're selling is popular in the beginning stages of your business.

Step 2: Build your meal plan! Ensure that all of the necessary nutrients are included inside of your meal plan and try to streamline your grocery list. The goal is to make a cost-effective meal plan that supplies a nice variety throughout the week! After you get your meal plans set up, it's time to move on to step3~!

Step 3: Start a Facebook Page and a Blog. Now's where the fun begins! It's time to set up a blog and a Facebook page for free! You can start a blog on one of the major blogging websites or you can purchase your own domain for $10, grab a free theme, and then set up some hosting for a couple of bucks. You're business is live and ready to rock. If you don't have $20, you can start your blog on a major blogging site. But be warned! Once your content goes on the website, it doesn't necessarily belong to you. It's highly recommended you start a website that you own, but there's nothing wrong with not having money to start off.

Step 4: Now that you have a platform to reach your customers, you can use your smart phone to begin your journey by making preparation videos for every meal inside of your weekly meal plan. Then at the end of the video, you can promote your meal plan services with included video descriptions! Over time, your customer base will build and you'll start to get a groove on meal planning business.

Step 5: After you get a little momentum moving, feel free to jump into your local community and join clubs, start classes at your home, and you can even offer a grocery delivery service where you bring groceries to your customer's doorstep with complete meal plans and other goodies!

2. **Start An Animal Service**

If you love animals and how adorable they are, you can begin your journey by offering a dog walking service and even start pet sitting while owners are away from home. Dog housing options aren't a pleasant thought for pet owners. They hate the thought paying a handful for their animals being locked up in a cage overnight. Today, the market isn't massive, but it's more than enough to find a couple of jobs to keep you busy. As you begin to generate money, you can offer to walk dogs while busy owners are at work and you can even begin taking in pets over the day. This may seem crazy, but some busy owner absolutely hate that to leave their pets home all day with no one to hangout with. On average, pet sitters make about $15 for every visit. This means that by visiting a dozen dogs a day, you'll be pulling in $180 for every day you work.

Steps to starting a pet sitting service.

Step 1: Do some research inside of your local market. You'll probably find some directories where there are care takers. Join a couple of sites and if you can't afford it, begin to ask around and talk to your friends. This will allow you to generate a couple of extra dollars so you can get a pet sitting certification and get yourself established on websites.

Step 2: Find your first job through asking around and dropping off some business cards with coupons for your first couple visits. Luckily, you can buy some business cards very cheap and you can set up a website where clients can visit. It does cost some money to buy those business cards, so you can use a free blogging site it will help you get the ball rolling in your local area. After you generate a couple of sales, you can create a professional website and join those pet sitter communities.

Step 3: After you get your first couple of customers, you can start a referral program that gives a free visit for every new customer that's referred.

Step 4: Learn which pet sitting directory is the most active inside of your area and exchange a free visit in exchange for a review from your current customer base. This will allow you to develop authority in the pet sitting space and will generate more income without investing more money in marketing.

You can make a pretty nice living through hanging out with wonderful animals. So if this seems like something for you, give it a shot! Hanging out with animals who enjoy your company is a pretty amazing way to start a pet business. After you start generating a good income, you can expand your company to start offering toys, services and more adventurous trips to the dog park!

3. Become A Social Media Consultant For Businesses In Your Area.

If you love spending your time on social media, you can use this to your advantage if you'd like to start a new business with very little money down. Social media consultants have a pretty cool job overall. The job is simple. To provide nice branding, increased exposure for small businesses, help customers who are frustrated, and to stimulate some buzz for the small business your working for.

It's actually pretty cheap to start up and it isn't an awful process to get started!

Social media consultants only need to spend about 5-10 hours a week to successfully impact the small business they work for and it's easy to charge $1,000/month for services.

Steps to Starting a Social Media Consulting Business:

Step 1: All you really need to get started in consulting is a computer and a phone. Check your local area for successful businesses who are lacking a social media presence and spend a couple of hours generating ideas to help the small business increase profits and exposure through social.

Step 2: After you've identified 5 businesses and built a plan to increase exposure, it's time to give them a call and visit them in store. In order to become successful, you'll probably need to invest your money in business cards and take some time up front to set up a local social media consulting profile and do everything you can to get your friends online to follow you.

Step 3: If you're struggling getting your first client, do some research online to build a more powerful case for your consulting services. You'll find tons of free information on successful local social consultants that are happy to share their information with others. Use what you can find for free to develop the most value you can develop for your company and begin to expand your role as a social media consultant.

Step 4: If you stay persistent, you'll be able to eventually find a business owner who understands the power of social media that doesn't have the time to address it. Once you get your first client, you can wait a couple of months and then offer the business $500 off a month for every new customer they refer to you. Over time, you'll have to pick up a new employee to help you with your work. You can expand your local services to include marketing, customer service handling and even branding.

4. Become a Senior Companion

If you enjoy kicking back with the older generation, the babies that were born shortly after World War II ended are starting to hang up the work suit to settle down into retirement. This leaves a huge opportunity for the people who enjoy helping others out. While this business can be a little competitive, there's a huge gap that's being created in supply and demand for the company. As a lot of people age, a lot of them start trying to stay out of senior communities, but they certainly want to stay active. By helping seniors get together and helping them in traveling to meet up with groups, you'll be able to spark a business with endless opportunities. Seniors have their money in place if they're set up in retirement which means that they're looking for ways to curb the pains of getting older.

You can offer senior services such as grocery delivery, home care and cleaning services. Over time, you'll find your schedule fills up pretty quickly and you'll make some kind friends in the process.

Steps to Becoming a Senior Companion:

Step 1: Ask around and get a feel for where seniors are spending their time. Drop a couple of business cards or venture over to a meet up group to sell your services.

Step 2: Get a vibe for what seniors who are actively spending money are looking for. Every city is different, but active seniors are a huge opportunity to generate income. Be kind, enjoy conversations and begin to understand what's plaguing the seniors in your area. If you think of a service you can offer seniors as their talking to you, give it a shot!

Step 3: Once you get your first customer, try to escort them over to meet up groups where they have some friends. This is a pretty cool way to develop a client base. You'll likely fill up your schedule quickly and you'll have to hire an employee to go shopping and do grocery deliveries while you escort your friends to their prized events.

Step 4: Build a brand that offers full services. Once you start filling up, you can buy a van and take a group of people on trips they cherish. Once you make friends with a group of seniors, your business will likely explode. Be prepared to hire new employees and to found a real business because if you enjoy this job, things will likely get crazy fast!

5. **Pick Up Tutoring & Teaching**

Not everyone understands a subject that you naturally grasp and they need help to understand a subject through a new perspective so they can get through school.

If you have a knack for science, language, history, or if you're just great at learning, teaching others can be the perfect place to start an information business. If you'd like to help others pass school, you can set up tutoring sessions and get paid handsomely for helping students pass your classes.

You can even offer classes in cooking, drawing, painting, technology, organization and parenting! Becoming a teach is a wonderful place to make some extra cash. If you hold 8 classes a month and you charge $25 per person, you'll make $2,000 a month if you attract 10 people for every class.

Steps To Becoming A Tutor Or Teacher:

Step 1: Identify what's going on around your community. What events get people together and what businesses have been busy lately.

Step 2: Think of classes and subjects that you can tutor inside of your active community. Then build a blueprint for teaching and even bring in some friends as well as renowned figure inside of your area.

Step 3: Build an online hub for your classes. You can create short videos and market your classes online to start generating buzz.

Step 4: Find authority figures that would like to teach. Start to build a schedule where major figures in your area are teaching your classes.

Step 5: Find a Venue. When you're starting a class, it's incredibly important to find a place to hold your class. If you've put in some hard work, you've likely set up a couple of dates where you have authority figures helping you with classes. When this happens, you've got the perfect product for a successful business to host. Your goal should be to hold your class at a local business that's been booming with business and to give them half of the revenue that you make during the class.

Step 6: You'll eventually start to gain traction with your business and you'll start generating a great following for your classes. Over time, you'll be able to sell some cool products and services that you can use to expand your business. All you have to do is pay attention to what your students are looking for and then supply them with the best solutions. For instance, you can get together with an authoritative sculptor and create a really cool DVD series you can sell for $100. Or you can simply sell sculpting tools to students who are consistently showing up to class.

6. Become an Event Planner.

There's a surprisingly pleasant job for you if you enjoy throwing parties. If you're crazy efficient, organized and you have a knack for throwing great events, this business is for you.

Event planning can range from publishing events, food drives, festivals, local concerts, formal parties, and weddings. The opportunities are endless if you love to throw parties and people always have a blast when you put something together.

You can even go as far as to plan group weekend getaways. No matter what you enjoy, there's probably a market for you.

Steps to Becoming an Event Planner.

Step 1: Start out by asking your friends if you can start throwing important events for them. You can start out by organizing baby showers, weddings, casual parties, celebrations, important milestones, and birthdays.

Step 2: Document the parties and begin to build a blog for your business. You can start off through using a free blog to show off your abilities to plan events. Over a couple of months, even if you haven't made much money through planning your events, you'll have a wonderful portfolio and you can begin to market it.

Step 3: Begin to research events that are happening in your area and start to capitalize off of that buzz. For example, if there's a local coffee shop that's making a killing off of open mic night, you can start a new one for a different coffee shop down the street. Make sure that there are no time conflicts and find open spots to begin to throw events. Over time, you'll begin to make companies money and you'll make a name for yourself. You'll begin to have people approaching you to plan events, activities and parties that are important to them and you'll begin to build consistent revenue.

Step 4: Begin marketing your services during your events. If you have 100 people attending an event, you'll likely run into one other person who's looking to throw an party for one reason or another. By sparking fun and exciting parties, you'll firmly establish your authority through how awesome your parties are. Before long, you'll be so busy, you'll need to hire someone to help you set up your events!

7. **Personal Trainer**

If you love fitness and health, you'll find yourself in the perfect position to become a personal trainer. The health of someone tends to be very important but sometimes people would like a pro to guide them along their journey to becoming more healthy. There are thousands of workout programs and diets, so people want someone who can design a personalized program. As a personal trainer, you get to work with people individually so they can accomplish your goals. If you have a nice track record for holding people accountable, this is probably the perfect job for you.

Step 1: Think of ways you can get your first client. Maybe you have a couple of friend or coworkers that need help or maybe you notice someone struggling at the gym. You can ever offer a service online for a personalized workout plan.

Step 2: Once you get results for one or two people, you can start asking for referrals and ask them for a testimonial you can share with others. You can then begin going to meet up groups that are related to the world of fitness.

You can join clubs that enjoy outdoor adventures, healthy cooking classes and even drop your card into healthy shops around town. Over time, you'll be able to get the ball rolling hey can show up, get to work and Health is a high priority for many, and losing weight and getting fit are top concerns in this area. If you have a track record for helping people with their fitness in a specific area, you could have a very profitable business.

Step 3: After your schedule starts to fill up, you can start hosting workout classes where people can show up for $10 a pop during week days and find fun ways to workout for

$25 during the weekends. If all goes well, you can host a workout class before work, a class after work, and launch 3 classes throughout the weekend. If you get an average attendance of 10 people per class, you'll be pulling in over $1,500 a week just by doing what you love. After you get some results for your classes, you can launch a video course and automate your income!

8. Get Paid To Inspire Others.

If you have a knack for living a pretty

awesome life, and you know how to inspire others to do the same, becoming a life coach might be the alley to start a business with no cost. If you can inspire, you can get paid pretty handsomely for increasing someone's quality of life. You can even choose to mentor others in your favorite hobbies like outdoor activities. One week, you can take a couple of people to go white water rafting and the next week, you'll help them conquer a mountain. The opportunities as a life coach are endless as long as the end result makes someone's life better. You can help anyone with business, happiness, dating, confidence, painting, singing and speaking. If there's a place where life can be improved, people would probably like to enjoy the same skills you have.

Steps to Becoming a Life Coach:

Step 1: Reflect around your community and look for rooms of opportunity and places that people are looking for help. Check out groups, businesses, and events to spark a couple of ideas for places to improve.

Step 2: Define the value of your inspiration. In order to inspire others, you have to connect to them on a deeper level. Without inspiration, nobody will want to pay for what you have to offer. So find out what sparks people's interest for a better future and then present your offer to help them create a life that they love. There's nothing more powerful than holding yourself accountable to an external source. If there's someone there holding you accountable, you're far more likely to succeed.

Step 3: Build a group of super achievers. Over the course of a couple months, you'll develop a pretty cool client base as you continue to help others achieve their goals for a better life. And the more people that get involved with your teachings, the more likely you are to be referred by your current customers.

9. **Start a Window Cleaning Business.**

The window cleaning business is actually a pretty easy business to start. All it takes is a little it of wit and an ability to walk into a store and ask if they'd like someone to clean their windows a couple times a week. Businesses only have one chance to build a first impression and the front of businesses have to stay clean in order to impress prospective customers and retain current ones. Starting a local window cleaning business doesn't necessarily sound like a dream business, but it's a perfect stepping stone if you'd like to get involved inside of marketing, branding and customer service.

Steps to Starting a Window Cleaning Business

Step 1: Find a spot in your local area filled with tons of small businesses. Try to avoid areas like shopping malls and look at shops that are locally owned and operated.

Step 2: Go scouting a couple of times a week and find a nice line of businesses that have dirty windows and offer to clean their windows. You can first offer strictly window cleaning packages. You can offer 2x a month, 1x a week, 3 times a week, and daily options with perks and benefits for each package.

Step 3: As your cleaning windows, remember that these businesses are locally operated and small business owners tend to be overwhelmed with tasks. Look around the shop and notice things that small business owners are falling behind on. Are shelves dusty? Is the company missing out on acquiring valuable emails? Are they missing something pivotal inside of their business? Or do they simply lack enough time to keep up with day to day business operations? Whatever you discover, there's always room to grow once you consistently show up to the front door of a small business.

Step 4: Get referrals by giving away a free week of the service that was referred. That means that if a company buys your Deluxe Cleaning Package, you give away a free week of the same package to the company that helped you acquired the business. Even if these businesses only get their windows cleaned twice a month, saying thank you for bringing in new business will revolutionize how quickly you expand your business. Before long, you'll have to hire on a couple of employees to help you operate you business day to day.

10.   Catering

If cooking is your specialty and you're not interested in starting a meal plan service or you just want to take you income to the next level, you can make a killing through catering special events in your community, business events, large parties, and gatherings. It can be a blast hosting your favorite foods for hundreds of people and the great news is that you get paid before you put together all of the food! This will allow you to cover up front food costs, help you hire a helping hand if you need it, and will give you a nice check for every meal that you cook.

Steps to Starting A Catering Business.

Step 1: Check out your local regulations for catering before you get started. Things can get a little complicated or you may need to buy a certification in order to start a catering business. However, most areas are pretty relaxed and your first catering service will more than pay for your

Step 2: Be mindful when creating your menu. Make sure you offer luxurious meals, but also be mindful to pick foods that will be liked by most people. Also look to maximize how little money you spend for each high quality meal that you create. If you can take a $4 meal and turn it around for $15, you'll make a killing if you cater for 100 people once a week.

Step 3: Look for opportunities where people need a ton of food. You can start by catering for weddings, formal parties, balls, and business outings. Simply contact businesses in your local area and introduce yourself. Over time, you'll find a couple of businesses who think your food looks way better than a bulk order of subway sandwiches.

Step 4: As you begin to make a little bit of income, start to take gambles inside of your business. Put your food in front of festivals, community events and local venues. Prepare to market your catering services and have a couple helpful hands with you. When you're looking to create exposure for your catering business, there's no better spot than putting your business in front of a thousand eyes. If your catering is heavily marketed like a giant sign that says "We Cater. Beef Tip Sandwiches $7." You'll be able to make short term money with long term perks.

11.   Start A Resume Writing Service.

People looking for high paying jobs encounter some epic competition. Resumes are the most important first impressions that hiring managers look at. To many potential candidates, the job they're applying for is a once in a lifetime opportunity for them to advance their career. However, if they aren't careful, their entire life's work can be dismissed in 5 seconds.

Having a properly formatted resume is the only way to earn an interview. If you take the time to understand what companies look for on successful resumes, you can make a wonderful income through helping other people get their dream jobs.

Steps To Starting A Resume Writing Service:

Step 1: Do your research on the technical aspects of resumes. Ensure that you are confident every one of your customers will pass through the initial 1st impression and that the resume guarantees the scheduling of an interview. In order to do this, you have to understand what hiring managers are looking for as they are inspecting the qualifications for their perspective employees.

Step 2: After you have a good grip on resumes, make some cards and drop them around local businesses even start a blog to help others build their resume. You can have a purchasing option for a custom made resume online. You can offer a phone call and then display your knowledge before asking the customers if they'd like you to build their resume. Resume writers typically net about $35,000 or more every year and can average well over $20/hour.

Step 3: Offer back end services to keep customers coming back. Someone who cares enough to get their resume professionally done is someone who is very conscious of their career and they aren't afraid to invest money to improve their careers. You can offer back end courses like time management consultation, boosting qualifications to improve income and even help someone advance far beyond their current pay grade.

Step 4: Like all the other businesses, once you get a couple of customers it's important to start generating referrals. If someone refers a new customer to you, you can give them cash incentives like $50 and a free time management consultation. This will allow you to get free customers at a discount and could even earn you some back end business!

12.   **Start a Writing Business.**

If you love reading or writing, starting a writing business can quickly become a profitable decision inside of your life. While there are avenues that requires thousands of dollars to get your writing career kicked off the ground, there's actually a couple of amazing ways you can start your business for free.

Steps To Starting A Writing Business:

Step 1: If you're looking to get payed to write, you're going to have to brush up on your grammar skills and crispen up your writing style. For the, it's recommended to get "The Only Grammar Book You'll Ever Need" and "The Elements of Style." If you're short on money, you can buy these books used for pretty cheap!

Step 2: After you get into a groove with your writing, it's time to apply to a couple of websites to get you started. It's highly recommended to do your research when you look for jobs. You can find sites that generate hundreds of dollars for your articles and you can find writing mills where you have non-stop access to thousands of articles across some wonderful niches.

Step 3: After you build your original portfolio, you should feel free to begin writing for your own blog, upgrading your pay through premium websites or even begin publishing your own books. These avenues tend to take months to develop, but the rewards for taking control over the content you produce are incredible.

13.   **Become A Tech Designer**

If you enjoy technology, you may have a future in designing websites, apps, games and software!Every month, there are thousands of businesses hiring skilled freelancers to produce gadgets to help run their business. If you like being around computers, this may be the perfect job for you! Some designers make a killing through software and website production. Local businesses would kill for a professional website at a nice price. If you'd like to design websites, you have a wonderful shot to make a wonderful income through local design.

Steps To Becoming A Tech Designer:

Step 1: Specialize in one specific language or skill as you start your tech business. Make sure you use one of the main coding languages and use your knowledge to build a nice portfolio through a couple of samples that your prospective clients can check out.

Step 2: After you have a few samples set up, it's time to rock! If you're looking for quick turnover time, website design is certainly the way to go.

Step 3: Get your first couple of clients through good old fashion marketing. Check around and do some research as you begin to sell the coding skill you've acquired. You can either contact businesses locally or you can find room for improvement over businesses that operate over the internet. Whatever route you choose, you have to make contact and let them know how valuable having whatever you're selling.

Step 4: Join a coding mill where business owners go to get technology built for them. There are hundreds of thousands of opportunities inside of coding and design online. Do some research and find a good website that has a nice stream of prospective clients so you can earn your first gig as a coder! Before long, you'll have some reviews rolling in and you'll be too busy to work alone. You'll have to hire on another coder before you know it.

The key is to work on your portfolio and get a few referrals under your belt. If you don't want to work with actual clients, you may want to instead consider using your design skills to create products such as business cards, website templates and stock illustrations that you can sell on sites such as Etsy.

14.   **Affiliate Marketing**

Selling someone's already successful products online is one of the easiest ways to build a business with almost no money down. If you enjoy a subject passionately, you can start your own website and social networking profiles and get to work!

Steps To Starting An Affiliate Marketing Business:

Step 1: Join an affiliate marketing community like clickbank to find successful products that you can market online. Once you found a profitable product you'd like to sell, you can move on to the next step.

Step 2: Buy your own domain and begin marketing your product(s). Buying a domain and hosting is pretty easy and you can just grab a free theme from wordpress to get your website launched with no coding experience.

Step 3: Begin to offer free information and relevant content across Twitter, Facebook and your website to build an initial flow of traffic. If you're struggling on how to get started, you can look at ways to generate followers online and discover ways to attract customers to your website.

Step 4: After you successfully sell your first product, you can expand your sales to other products and even invest in paid advertising to generate more traffic.

15.   **Start A Logo Design Business.**

If you enjoy graphic design, you can make tons of money online and throughout your local community. Logo design, is a quick way to build your design portfolio and it's very easy to start up. If you're looking for a creative outlet, this is the perfect way for you to get started on any big dream.

Steps To Stating A Logo Design Business:

Step 1: Join a website that hosts logo designs. Most of these sites are free and after you earn profits, they charge you a fee in exchange for your work. It's a pretty fun way to make money and it costs no money up front.

Step 2: As you begin building your local designs online, you can start looking around your local community with your portfolio. You can ask local businesses if they're interested in having a logo designed for them and you can charge them a modest fee for your work.

Step 3: After you start getting a client base, you can expand your business from logos to banners, flyers, and even mobile layouts. Graphic designers have an unlimited opportunity once they get their foot inside of the industry. Once you start filling out your income, try new ways to express your creative side and look for ways to improve your income for every project you do!

These 15 businesses can all be started for $20 or less. The only investments required in starting these companies is in purchasing business cards or websites to allow your business to be seen by your prospective customers. Anything can be done through action in today's economy. All it takes is a little bit of confidence and a smooth but systematic approach to getting your first customer. Once you have a couple of clients, most businesses tend to take off through referrals and cheap exposure strategies.

There's no limits to the amount of money you can make when you start a business. If you're interested in starting a business, now is your chance to get things rolling. Don't spend your time dwelling on whether or not these businesses will work if you try them out. Get out and try to start your favorite business and have a blast doing something you're passionate about for your job. If you put in the hard work up front, you'll quickly find that you can replace your income and you'll be able to shift into your job full time!

Have fun and if there's any point in time where you hit a snag when you're starting up, just look online for free recommendations for the situation that you're encountering. Everything you need to become successful is free online. Good resources for help starting a business are loaded throughout the internet. So don't fret about whether or not you think you can succeed inside of business .

Taking action is the only way you can successfully make your dreams a reality. Every strategy presented in this book is simplistic but effective and will guide you through your first sale. 90% of most aspiring entrepreneurs never make it to their first sale, but if you take action and stay patient you'll find that your business will start to gain traction and you'll begin to make a living from your business.

Now that money isn't an issue for you to get started, what's stopping you? Have fun with your $20 Start Up, and feel free to share your success stories!

www.ingramcontent.com/pod-product-compliance
Lightning Source LLC
Chambersburg PA
CBHW061442180526
45170CB00004B/1517